ON THE SPECTRUM OF POSSIBLE DEATHS

LUCIA PERILLO

On the
Spectrum of
Possible Deaths

Copper Canyon Press
Port Townsend, Washington

Cover art: Giotto di Bondone, detail from
The Last Judgement, ca. 1305.

Photo credit: Alinari/Art Resource, NY.

Copper Canyon Press is in residence at
Fort Worden State Park in Port Townsend,
Washington, under the auspices of Centrum.
Centrum is a gathering place for artists and
creative thinkers from around the world,
students of all ages and backgrounds, and
audiences seeking extraordinary cultural
enrichment.

LIBRARY OF CONGRESS
CATALOGING-IN-PUBLICATION DATA
Perillo, Lucia Maria, 1958-
On the spectrum of possible deaths /
Lucia Perillo.
    p.   cm.
ISBN 978-1-55659-397-0 (hardback)
I. Title.

PS3566.E69146O5 2012
811´.54—dc23

                                    2011050110

98765432 FIRST PRINTING

COPPER CANYON PRESS
Post Office Box 271
Port Townsend, Washington 98368
www.coppercanyonpress.org

For all the Roberts

ACKNOWLEDGMENTS

Grateful acknowledgment is made to the
editors of the following publications, in
which these poems first appeared:

*The American Poetry Review, The Atlantic,
Barrow Street, Kenyon Review Online, The
Los Angeles Review, New England Review,
The New Yorker, Orion, Ploughshares, Poetry,
Rio Grande Review, Salt Hill, Seneca Review,
Southern California Review, Subtropics,
Tin House,* and *Voices in Italian Americana.*

No death for you. You are involved.

WELDON KEES

CONTENTS

ON THE SPECTRUM OF POSSIBLE DEATHS

The Second Slaughter

Achilles slays the man who slew his friend, pierces the corpse
behind the heels and drags it
behind his chariot like the cans that trail
a bride and groom. Then he lays out
a banquet for his men, oxen and goats
and pigs and sheep; the soldiers eat
until a greasy moonbeam lights their beards.

The first slaughter is for victory, but the second slaughter is for grief—
in the morning more animals must be killed
for burning with the body of the friend. But Achilles finds
no consolation in the hiss and crackle of their fat;
not even heaving four stallions on the pyre
can lift the ballast of his sorrow.

And here I turn my back on the epic hero—the one who slits
the throats of his friend's dogs,
killing what the loved one loved
to reverse the polarity of grief. Let him repent
by vanishing from my concern
after he throws the dogs onto the fire.
The singed fur makes the air too difficult to breathe.

When the oil wells of Persia burned I did not weep
until I heard about the birds, the long-legged ones especially
which I imagined to be scarlet, with crests like egrets
and tails like peacocks, covered in tar
weighting the feathers they dragged through black shallows
at the rim of the marsh. But once

I told this to a man who said I was inhuman, for giving animals
my first lament. So now I guard
my inhumanity like the jackal
who appears behind the army base at dusk,
come there for scraps with his head lowered
in a posture that looks like appeasement
though it is not.

Again, the Body

*I have become what I have always been and it
has taken a lifetime, all of my own life, to reach
this point where it is as if I know finally that I
am alive and that I am here, right now.*

TOBIAS SCHNEEBAUM, *Keep the River on
Your Right*

When you spend many hours alone in a room
you have more than the usual chances to disgust yourself—
this is the problem of the body, not that it is mortal
but that it is mortifying. When we were young they taught us
do not touch it, but who can keep from touching it,
from scratching off the juicy scab? Today I bit
a thick hangnail and thought of Schneebaum,
who walked four days into the jungle
and stayed for the kindness of the tribe—
who would have thought that cannibals would be so tender?
This could be any life: the vegetation is thick
and when there is an opening, you follow
down its tunnel until one night you find yourself
walking as on any night, though of a sudden your beloved
friends are using their stone blades
to split the skulls of other men. Gore everywhere,
though the chunk I ate was bland;
it was only when I chewed too far and bled
that the taste turned satisfyingly salty.
How difficult to be in a body,
how easy to be repelled by it,
eating one-sixth of the human heart.
Afterward, the hunters rested

their heads on one another's thighs
while the moon shined on the river
for the time it took to cross the narrow sky
making its gash through the trees…

My Father Kept the TV On

while the books lay open, scattered facedown
like turtles sunning, the jackets hunched, with a little
hump in the hunch from the trough of the spine,
bearing a white sticker with the typewriter's Courier
font rendition of the decimal system
under the wrapper, hazy like fog
taped to the book, the tape's yellow orange-almost
(depending on how old) reinforced with threads.

Meanwhile his eyes drifted back and forth
back and forth until the book slid to the floor.
The flag then. Then snow. Or the corporate logo
of the eye—all night the night would watch him,
plural, *them*. Just ask my friend whose father
was a drunk, a highball glass on the nightstand and a swizzle
stick to mark his place. Still, on Thursday nights
he stumbled down to the reading room
to leaf through the new arrivals.

Oh green republic where the pilgrims came to land!
If I'm going to choose my nostalgia it is a no-brainer
that I'm going to side with books, with the days
before the lithium-ion battery, but after
Philip Roth and John le Carré were born, books not too
highbrow or too low, but sometimes thick
and overdue. Books the fathers read to escape us
who were the shackles that the plodding days
latched on to them who'd started out their lives with war, so this

was perfect, courting danger in their underwear,
feeling the breast of the vixen stiffen,
slipping their hands into the thief's black glove.

After the Names Are Gone, the Damage Will Remain

Though the twins were not identical, they both had skin
so thin & clear I could see their veins' squiggling underneath.
One with red hair, one with white

& the veins made their combined colors patriotic
if a little terrifying
in the auditorium where we'd assembled,

their tears falling in a formal style of grief
reserved for civic purposes, I learned this
from mothers who'd stood by the mailbox, weeping

as we filed by them in the school bus
six years before, when bullets ruined the famous head
of the famous handsome man. Now

the girls' red eye-rims similarly deliquesced,
their shrill notes ascending:
President Eisenhower! Has! Died!

news that made me scratch an old mosquito bite
& scrutinize the upturned faces of my shoes—
even in my girlish nerdfog

I must have understood that some will not withstand posterity,
that all the bodies on the beach at Normandy
still lead to the muse's turning her cool marble shoulder.

Permissible to insert here the twins' white lashes
& the curve of their hot foreheads. But
how tentatively one must ask the nouns & verbs

to step apart for Eisenhower, though he ransacked
more than his share of cities. Like the moon
his pale head hovers, yet he does not go around

like some transhistorical Fuller Brush man
sticking his foot in the door
the pale girl of my ode slams shut.

To the Field of Scotch Broom That Will Be Buried by the New Wing of the Mall

Half costume jewel, half parasite, you stood
swaying to the music of cash registers in the distance
while a helicopter chewed the linings
of the clouds above the clear-cuts.
And I forgave the pollen count
while cabbage moths teased up my hair
before your flowers fell apart when they
turned into seeds. How resigned you were
to your oblivion, unlistening to the cumuli
as they swept past. And soon those gusts
will mill you, when the backhoe comes
to dredge your roots, but that is not
what most impends, as the chopper descends
to the hospital roof so that somebody's heart
can be massaged back into its old habits.

Mine went a little haywire
at the crest of the road, on whose other side
you lay in blossom.
As if your purpose were to defibrillate me
with a thousand electrodes,
one volt each.

The Caucus

I had my precinct wrong and went to Garfield Elementary
where the hall monitors would not let me through

because I live on the wrong side of the boundary. I could hear
my neighbors, listening reasonably to one another,

listening even to the man who is my adversary
because he leaves his dog's crap on the sidewalk's grassy strip.

If he wants to fly, Peter Pan has to focus very hard on Tinker Bell.
If he is quiet and he concentrates, then he can fly.

The girl who spoke sat in the hallway,
so I asked if she was working on her reading. "No,

she's autistic those are her socialization cards," said her mother,
who asked if I would watch her girl (whose name was Terri)

so she (the mother)
could take part in the caucus.

He can fly only when he focuses on Tinker Bell.
He can focus only when he listens.

In the classrooms, my neighbors sat in chairs
that shrank their knee-chin distance pitifully. I heard my adversary

say he didn't think the candidate looked authentic enough
and that's how history gets made. Quick

write it down before it slips
too far downstream.

Peter Pan likes to sing and hear Tinker Bell sing.
When he hears Tinker Bell sing, Peter Pan is happy.

In the classroom, something was decided—
I heard the collective exhale of assent

before people filed out, looking giddy and grave. When she returned
I asked Terri's mother what was up

with the singing, and she said that other children
tormented her girl with songs.

Go tell that to a poet.
It would explain a lot about the current state of the art.

Orpheus sang,
and, like the Beatles, his song made the girls scream

so loud they drowned the song. Then they yelled
See yonder our despiser and tore off his head.

Peter Pan and Tinker Bell like to sing together.
They are very happy when they sing.

You know one girl alone wouldn't have done it,
and this is not just a matter of strength. There's a fuse

running from one of us to the other—lucky thing
all that's in my pocket is this old packet

of moist towelettes
I mistook for a matchbook.

She thanked me, the mother, even though Terri
had been reading her cards to my dog. Note

I carry a blue (biodegradable and perfumed)
plastic crap bag, though it hadn't been used yet,

there at the school, and I was letting it flap
from the pocket of my red flannel shirt

like the American flag.
Come, my adversary—

let us discuss the warblers.
How sweetly they torment us from the budding trees.

Domestic

Here the coyote lives in shadows between houses,
feeds by running west to raid the trash behind the store
where they sell food that comes in cans
yesterday expired. Picture it
perching on the dumpster, a corrugated
sheet of metal welded to the straight, its haunch
accruing the imprint of the edge until it pounces,
skittering on the cans. It has tried
to gnaw them open and broken all its teeth.

Bald-flanked, rheumy-eyed, sniffing the wheels
of our big plastic trash carts but too pigeon-
chested to knock them down, scat full of eggshells
from the compost pile. "I am like that, starved,
with dreams of rutting in a culvert's narrow light—"
we mumble our affinities as we vacate into sleep.
Because we occupy the wrong animal—don't you too feel it?
Haven't you stood in the driveway, utterly confused?
Maybe you were taking out the garbage, twisting
your robe into a noose-knot at your throat, when you stopped
fighting the urge to howl, and howled—
and did it bring relief, my friend, however self-deceiving?

Skedans

I paddled many days to reach the totem poles
not barged off to Vancouver. Tilting in a clearing,
gray and cracked, upholding the clouds,
the grain for a hundred years having risen.
The ghosts of Cumshewa Inlet kept trying to evict me,
but I did not want to leave
because the Haida had left their dead here
and once you step over a human bone while following a deer-path
you want to step over another, unless you are not ruled
by curiosity as I was ruled. Or had already seen a skull
mossy in its entirety, with three holes (eye sockets
+ the nose) + the palate on the duff.
Into which the green teeth bit, the moss
covering it all like luminescent car upholstery,
what do you do if you are just a dumb American,
I can usually figure out how to behave, but require years
to come to my conclusions. Now
the fact the reparations have come due
is being made clear by the photo of the skull
I took when I was young and dumb, this anti-
luck charm emanating green recriminations,
though I notice that I do not take it from the wall.

I Could Name Some Names

of those who have drifted through thus far of their allotted
fifty or seventy or ninety years on Earth
with no disasters happening,
whatever had to be given up was given up—
the food at the rehab facility was better than you would expect
and the children turned out more or less okay;
sure there were some shaky years
but no one's living in the basement anymore
with a divot in his head, that's where the shrapnel landed/or
don't look at her stump. It is easy
to feel possessed of a soul that's better schooled
than the fluffy cloud inside of people who have never known suchlike
events by which our darlings
are unfavorably remade. And the self
is the darling's darling
($I = darling^2$). Every day
I meditate against my envy
aimed at those who drift inside the bubble of no-trouble,
—what is the percentage? 20% of us? 8%? zero?
Maybe the ex-president with his nubile daughters,
vigorous old parents, and clean colonoscopy. Grrrr.
Remember to breathe. *Breathe in suffering,*
breathe out blessings say the ancient dharma texts.
Still I beg to file this one complaint
that some are mountain-biking through the scrublands
while she is here at Ralph's Thriftway,
running her thumb over a peach's bruise,
her leg a steel rod
in a miniskirt, to make sure I see.

Cold Snap, November

That we find a crystal or a poppy beautiful
means that we are less alone, that we are more
deeply inserted into existence than the course of
a single life would lead us to believe.
JOHN BERGER, *The Sense of Sight*

In 2006, in Ohio, Joseph Clark raised his head in
the middle of his execution to say, "It's not working."

The salmon corpses clog the creek without sufficient room to spin:
see, even the fish want to kill themselves this time of year
the therapist jokes. Her remedy
is to record three gratitudes a day—
so let the fish count for one, make two the glaucous gulls
who pluck the eyes before they fill
with the cloudy juice of vanishing.

But don't these monuments to *there*-ness
feel a little ostentatious? Not just the gratitudes,
but also what they used to call a hardware store
where you hike for hours underneath the ether
between the ceiling and the dropped-down lighting tubes,
muttering *I need a lock-washer for my lawnmower shroud*—
huh? You know
you should feel like Walt Whitman, celebrating
everything, but instead you feel like Pope Julius II
commanding Michelangelo to carve forty statues for his tomb.

When even one giant marble Moses feels like a bit too much.

This year made it almost to December without a frost to deflate the dahlias
and though I stared for hours at the psychedelia of their petals,
trying to coax them to apply their shock-paddles to my heart,
it wasn't working. Until one morning when
I found them black and staggering in their pails,
charred marionettes, twist-tied to their stakes, I apologize
for being less turned-on by the thing than by its going.
Not the sunset
but afterward when we stand dusted with the sunset's silt,

and not the surgical theater, even with its handsome anesthesiologist
in blue dustcap and booties—no,

his *after*'s what I'm buzzed by, the black slide into nothing
(well, someone ought to speak for it).

Or it can come in white—not so much the swirling snow
as the fallen stuff that makes the mind continuous
with the meadow that it sees.

Auntie Roach

Courage is no good:
It means not scaring others.

PHILIP LARKIN

One day George Washington rides around Mount Vernon
for five hours on his horse, the next
he's making his auspicious exodus
on the spectrum of possible deaths.
Rasputin was fed cyanide in little cakes
but did not slough his living husk,
and so Prince Felix sang to him, then mesmerized him
with a gaudy cross. And though he dropped when he was shot
he popped back up and ran outside: it was
Purishkevich who fired three times in the courtyard—
but even with his body bound
in the frozen Neva, one arm worked

its way free. Now, he must have howled
while his giblets leaked, though the cold
is reputed to be kind. Sliding his end
toward a numeral less horrible; it falls
say as a six on a scale of zero to ten?
Shakespeare went out drinking, caught a fever,
ding! Odds are we'll be addled—
what kind of number can be put on that?
One with endless decimals,
unless you luck into some kind woman,
maker of the minimum wage, black or brown and brave enough
to face your final wreck? My friends horde pills

for their bad news, but I wonder if it's cowardly
to be unequal to the future. Someone should write a book
for nursery school, with crucial facts like: how,
as the sun drops, shadows lengthen, including a sharp
or blurry one that is your own. And you scuttle from it
like a cockroach fleeing light—an anti-roach,
running from the dark. See my feelers, long and feathery:
I am more than well prepared.
Ulysses Grant lay in misery for half a year,
after eating a peach that pained his tongue.
Versus Ivan the Terrible, last heard singing in the bath,
who fainted dead while setting up the chessboard.

Another Treatise on Beauty

The boyish foreign tyrant wears faun-colored desert boots
hooked boyishly around the rungs of his chair

on this talk show where he speaks with the voice of a woman
who interprets from the ether. He's smiling

like the naughty boy in school who picked his teeth
with a stiletto: mister, you may be despicable

but my boyfriend wore those same boots once,
and I loved him in them, despite the stolen tape deck

in his car. How small a blemish does your narco-trafficking
shrink to, what with that comely stubble on your cheeks,

your brocade cap and wool cape tossed
across your shoulder like a cavalier's? Perhaps we need

to recalibrate the scale or set your crimes
in one pan of the balance, so when we set your beauty

in the other it will rise, as beauty does, instead of clunking down.
As beauty rises, even when it goes unseen. See

how many of the famous modern paintings
were made by men who have such vigor in old age?

And when I flip open the back covers of their books,
the famous lady poets all have shiny hair.

Bad French Movie

Isabelle Huppert in a peep show booth
with the wilted bloom of a used Kleenex,
and not her Kleenex, *une mouchoir étrange*—
this is not a promising get-go.

But can't my hopes be phototropic
as I sit in the front row with my head cocked back
like a newly fractured dicotyledonous bean
uncurling on its sprout?

The popcorn here is not just bad—
for years the hopper has accrued its crud
so that sometimes you crunch down on what
tastes like a greasy tractor bolt

and are transported to a former Soviet republic
instead of some seedy part of Paris.
You have to swipe the burned nib off your lips
before scuffing it back, toward the lovers who've come

to make out in this habitat, upholstered
in the velvet mode of tongues. And when
I turn to see if they've noticed
their ankles' being pinged by my scorched old maids

all the hardware bolted in their faces
glints like moonlight on the road after the crash is cleared away,
as the projector beam keeps on doggedly charging
through a googolplex of twitching motes.

Giving us Isabelle unclothed again,
Isabelle in the tones of the wood of a cello,
Isabelle if you're trying to save us now
all your skin is not enough.

Proximity to Meaningful Spectacle*

Monday
       Wednesday
              Friday,
I swim with the old ladies, hurry:

the synchronized swimming team arrives at three.
       We ride the wacky noodles
              through blue pastures
lit by chemicals—

I like to go under in my goggles
       to watch their them-ness bleed
              into my me
until we are evicted by the lifeguard, Danielle.

In the locker room, some retreat into the changing stalls
       to sequester their mastectomies,
              but your walker will not fit there, no;
you have to peel your swimsuit in the open

with the girls on the team. I'm staring
       at one long strip of mostly leg,
              daring her to
reciprocate:

but all this future-flesh has made her shy—
       the way the belly sometimes flabs from having kids

*Joe Wenderoth

and doubles down.
I thought this was a them-trait, not a me-trait,

but was mistaken about the boundary—
      which turns out not to be a wall, but a net
            in which we each hang like a sausage
in a shop window, liquefying in the sun.

Good luck synchro girl, trying to wriggle
      into your spangly suit
            without taking off your bra—
not wanting any of your you to bleed into your me

as you reach around yourself to pull out what you pull out
      by the scruff of its neck:
            your limp blue animal
of lace.

Hokkaido

War Emblem, the famous stallion,
will not mount a female rump
on the island of Hokkaido
in a pasture near the sea.
It is hard to imagine anyone not being overcome
by the sight of two dozen mares
surrounded by volcanoes (is the problem
that the metaphors are too direct?), and yet
War Emblem is still not in the mood.

A thousand years ago the courtesan Shikibu
wrote a thousand poems to her lover,
the references to sex made tasteful through concision
and the image of their kimonos intertwined.
Either her heart was broken or it was full,
either way required some terse phrases to the moon.

Was that all it was? Dumb animal hunger?
All those years when I thought I was making Art
out of The One Important Thing?
And how to apologize now for my lack of adequate concision?
Once I was so full of juice and certain of its unending.

At the Hatchery

The woman who wears dark glasses large as goggles
has her hand wrapped around the elbow of the young woman
who is beautiful. Where does it come from,
this compulsion not just to know their thinking

but to live inside her for a while, the one
whose eyes are hidden as she looks
down into the impoundment where the salmon who've swum upriver
end their travels? It must sound large to her, the clang

a loose piece of metal makes against the cement wall
whenever a fish leaps in its fury, I am claiming
the privilege to impute its fury as we listen to them
thrash. Dozens were killed an hour ago

because their future fate is better if the eggs are stripped
than if they're left to their fandango
in the frothing of the creek. I have tried to live inside them too,
these fish who strain against the world, or into it, why

am I not so intent on battling my way into the young woman
who moves from one thing to another without hurry?
I would eavesdrop, but they talk in Spanish,
thwarting my attempt to learn if the blind woman can detect

the coolness radiating from the pile of slush, all that remains
of the ice in which the dead were packed
before being trucked off to the food bank: if she could see
she'd see the vapor rising, as from a fire not quite put out.

Victor the Shaman

I feel the need for more humanity
because the winter wren is not enough,
even with its complicated music emanating

from the brambles. So I relent to my friend
who keeps bugging me to see her shaman,
tutored by the Indians who live at the base

of Monte Albán. Tutored also by the heavy bag
at Sonny's Gym: *Box like heaven / Fight like hell*
his T-shirt says; the graphic shows an angel's fist

buried to the wrist in Satan's brisket, while the prince
of dark jabs the angel's kisser. Victor
has sandpiper legs, his ponytail a mess of webs,

but he has eaten the ayahuasca vine
and chanted in the sweat lodge
and entered the fight-cage in a bar in Tucson,

Adam's apple jiggling his Star of David
when he writes me out a prayer.
He says he flew here to visit his grandma,

only she died before the plane touched down—
the dead leave yard sales to the living,
who shoot staple guns at telephone poles

and soothe their eyes with slabs of meat.
No matter how many rounds you go in practice,
he says you always come out unprepared

om ah hum
vajra siddhi padma hum

for the mountain of junk inside the house: cedar canoe
in the rafters and the box of Kotex he found
from her last menstrual period in the 1950s.

Wheel

I sat, as I do, in the shallows of the lake—

after crawling through the rotting milfoil on the shore.
At first
the materials offered me were not much—

just some cattails where a hidden bullfrog croaked
and a buckhouse made from corrugated tin—

at first I thought I'd have to write the poem of its vapors.
But wait
long enough and the world caves in,

sends you something like these damselflies
prickling your chest. And the great ventriloquist
insists

you better study them or else:

how the liquidmetal blue gleams like a motorcycle helmet,
how the markings on the thorax wend like a maze,

their abdomens ringed like polecat tails,
the tip of his latched
to the back of her neck

while his scrawny forelegs wipe his mandible
that drops and shuts like a berth on a train.

But when I tallied his legs, he already had six—

those wiper-legs belonged to a gnat
he was cramming in his mouth. Which took a long time

because the gnat struggled, and I tried to imagine
a gnat-size idea of the darkness
once the mandible closed.

Call me bad gnat: see how every other thing strives—
more life!
Even with just two neurons firing the urge.

Then the she-fly's abdomen swung forward
to take the sperm packet from his thorax,
and he finished chewing

in this position that the field guide calls *The Wheel*.

Call me the empress of the unused bones,
my thighs fumigated by the rank detritus of the shore

while the meal
and The Wheel
interlocked in a chain

in the blue mouth of the sky
in the blacker mouth beyond

while I sat, as I do, in the shallows of the lake
where sixty thousand damselflies

were being made a half-inch from my heart.

After Reading *The Tibetan Book of the Dead*

The hungry ghosts are ghosts whose throats
stretch for miles, a pinprick wide,
so they can drink and drink and are never sated.
Every grain of sand is gargantuan
and water goes down thick as bile.

I don't know how many births it takes to get
reborn as not the flower but the scent.
To be allowed to exist as air (a prayer
to whom?)—dear whom:
the weight of being is too much.

Victor Feguer, for his final meal,
asked for an olive with a pit
so that a tree might sprout from him.
It went down hard, but now the murderer is comfort.
He is a shady spot in the potter's field.

But it must be painful to be a tree,
to stand so long with your arms up.
You might prefer to be a rock
(if you can wear that heavy cloak).
In Bamiyan, the limestone Buddhas stood

as tall as minor mountains, each one carved
in its own alcove. Their heads
eroded over time, and the swallows
built nests from their dust,
even after zealots blew them up.

Now the swallows wheel in empty alcoves,
their mouths full of ancient rubble.
Each hungry ghost hawks up his pebble
so he can breathe. And the dead
multiply under the olive tree.

The Black Rider

There are blows in life, so powerful…
I don't know!

CESAR VALLEJO, TRANS. CLAYTON ESHLEMAN

Driving past the Masonic graveyard, I see a boy
skateboarding down the new asphalt of the walk
that he veers off so he can jump
and slide along a tombstone.

He has such faith in the necklace of his bones
he will not let a helmet wreck his hair—
why does the brain have to be buried
in the prettiest place? You little shit, don't you know

someone slaved at the brewery to pay for what was
supposed to stand as shiny as your hair
two centuries or three, when all your ollies
will no longer stir a moth or midge?

But what kind of grump would rather be eaten
by wind and rain than the glissando of a punk
riding off with a whump to the door of the oven
with a few bright flakes of someone else's death?

Pioneer

Let's not forget the Naked Woman is still out there, etched
into her aluminum plaque
affixed to her rocket
slicing through the silk of space.
In black and white, in *Time*, we blast her

off to planets made of gases and canals,
not daring to include, where her legs fork,
the little line to indicate she is an open vessel.
Which might lead to myths about her
being lined with teeth,

knives, snakes, bees—an armament
flying through the firmament. Beside the man
who stands correctly nonerect, his palm
upraised to show he comes in peace,
though you globulous yet advanced beings

have surely taken a gander of our sizzling planet
and can see us even through our garments.
So you know about the little line—
how a soft animal cleaves from her
and how we swaddle it in fluff,

yet within twenty years we send it forth
with a shoulder-mounted rocket-propelled-grenade launcher:
you have probably worked out a theory
to explain the transformation. And you
have noticed how she looks a bit uncertain

as she stands on her right leg, her left thrust out
as if she's put her foot on top of something
to keep it hidden. Could be an equation
on a Post-it, or could be a booby trap—
now comes time to admit we do not know her very well, she

who has slipped the noose of our command. Be careful
when you meet her, riding on her shaft of solar wind:
you will have to break her like a wishbone
to get her open, she whom we filled with teeth
and knives and snakes and bees.

Fireball

The TV knob was made of resin, its gold skirt
like a Kewpie doll's, but it was gone.
So we changed the channel
with a pair of pliers (on the flat spot
on the spindle): chunk chunk
and then lo, Jerry Lewis. Chunk chunk and lo,
the marionettes with giant hands. The song went:
my heart would be a fireball. And in the chunking
and the singing and the watching, lo, my heart became one.

Less pageantry in the now. Say *Sputnik*: no other word
climbs my throat with such majestic flames.
Gone, the marionettes in flightsuits made of foil
gone grainy on the boob tube. The tremulous way
their bodies moved, my fear for their well-being.
The comic stupidity of the child,
which is forgiven. Unlike the stupidities to come.

The boy had a guinea pig named Fireball, so I taught him
the song by way of mourning
when it died. He still possessed his sweetness,
unlike older sons who think you are a moron without big
subwoofers in your car. To that son I say:
you may think you're one of the alpha-carnivores
just because you've shot many avatars of whores

on a video screen that you will never have the Cuban missile crisis on;
you do not even really have the bomb, and how can anyone
command their cool without the bomb: Sam Cooke, James Dean,

those boys lived kitty-corner to their annihilation.
But my son glazes—what's so special about the past
when everyone has one? And yours, he says,
is out of gas. Then vroom, he's off—
you might think his car is breathing by the way the windows
bend. Welcome to the new world, Mom,
he says, if you hear singing, it ain't a song.

To Carlos Castaneda

After the physics final, Gina and I, in our mukluks
scuffed past the swanky shops on Sherbrooke
then climbed the mountain in the city. December 5,
1975: I tried to will myself to have a vision, though the stars
would not cooperate—instead of a sweat lodge
or a kiva, the warm-up hut at the top of Mount Royal
looked completely un-aboriginal, a replica in miniature
of the Château de Versailles. With night all around us
cold and thick as glass, I don't know how the starlight
managed to pass through it to sting me, it was hard enough
to lift my hand to knock the door, a joke,
it was so late. And here past the midpoint of my life
I think I'll die without a paranormal apparition
to which I could wholeheartedly attest. I am not sure
I even have a soul, a corny soul, a little puppet
made of cream and feathers. Yet the door
did open (turned out to be only six p.m.)
and the old man said, *Ah jeunes filles, il paraît que vous
avez froid.* Then he unstacked two chairs and set them
down before the fire, still chewing its meal of logs
in the giant hearth. Inside the château of our silence,
we sat and chewed our lips: wasn't the sacred knowledge
supposed to involve telepathy with animals, and astral travel
to planets made of light? Kindness (b) seemed too corny
to be the answer (*Restez ici pour le temps que vous
voudrez*) though we were given no other choice
except (a) his sweeping, and (c) the mice inside the walls.

300D

When he was flush, we ate dinner
at Tung Sing on Central Avenue
where my father liked the red-dye-number-toxic
bright and shiny food: spareribs, sweet-
and-sour pork—what else
was there to care about, except his sleep
under the pup tent of the news? And the car,
which was a Cadillac until he saw how they
had become the fortresses of pimps—
our hair may look stylish now,
but in the photograph it always turns against us:
give it time and it will turn. Maybe it was in 1976
he went to see the enemy, the man
(with sideburns) who sold German cars
and said: take it easy, step at a time,
see how the diesel motor sounds
completely different. So off he went tink-tink-tink
around the block in the old neighborhood
where he imagined people (mostly black: by now
his mouth had mastered the word's exhale,
then cut) lifting their heads to look (-*kuh*).
And he, a short man, sat up taller as he swung
back into the lot to make the deal, although
to mitigate the shift in his allegiances
(or was this forgiveness?—for the Germans
had bombed his boat as he sailed through Gibraltar)
he kept the color constant. *Champagne,*
the color of a metal in a dream, no metal
you could name, although they tried

with a rich man's drink. He could afford it now
though it made him feel a little silly, his hand a lump
of meat around the glass's narrow, girlish stem.

Photograph: The Enemy

Great-Uncle Stefan wears the Austro-Hungarian Empire's sailor suit,
its cap flat and black, his long
dark hair pomaded in a stiff
blunt skirt behind his neck.
There's something about the nose's
bulb-and-nostril conglomeration that we share,
and though I'm not a man I like to think
I am a sailor, with a waxed moustache like his
whose curled-up ends provide
an occupation for our nervous hands,
twirling it so as not to betray
with a squint or smirk his sympathies,
which lie with the murderer Princip.
Who shot the Archduke in Sarajevo, where
it took me a long time in the assassination museum,
reading Cyrillic via the osmotic method
of translation, before I figured out
Princip was the hero of the place: a person
could match her feet with his imprinted
in the sidewalk and pull the trigger of her fingers.
And enter the fantasy of being The One Who Caused
The Greater Past, which I could not resist:
my knuckle crooked, and clicked.
However I did spare the Duchess Sophie.

Photograph: Grandfather, 1915

It's the Bronx, Barretto Point, so the sea
cannot be far away. But all we have to go on
is the lone pine in the distance—the rest
bleached by the chemistry of time. Also
there's this young man in the foreground, squatting
with his forearms balanced on the fulcrum of his knees,
speaking to what's disappeared. It is a blur
resembling a woman with her arm extended,
urging him to follow. Soon the Great Depression
will also call him, and for lack of other work
will send him downstairs to the boiler
where he'll nurse the chromosome of sadness
while his words turn into coal. But he was not really
down there with the onions and potatoes—
in a moment, he will follow her
into the waters off Barretto Point, which will turn his good white shirt
translucent. Like the translucence he was led by,
but in this picture he hasn't risen yet
to cross the muddy shoreline. He's still crouched
in the upland, growing misty with the nebula who touches him,
misty at the prospect of his likewise turning into mist
as the camera makes this record of their betrothal.

Gleaner at the Equinox

Dusk takes dictation from the houses.
Sometimes sobs and sometimes screams—
laughter, too, though it doesn't settle like the others
into the hollows of the Virgin Mary's face.

In her concrete gown, she's standing by
the satellite dish absorbing for the trailer on the corner,
wearing shoulder pads of Asian pears I stole some of
before the windfall fell. When the dog
lifts his leg to soil a withered rose I say *Good boy.*

Nightshade vines overtake the house of the widow,
their flowers turned into yellow berries
that there are no birds in nature idiot enough
to mistake for food.

after Dick Barnes

Lubricating the Void

Heidemarie Stefanyshyn-Piper: I can barely pronounce your name
but have been thinking of you ever since your grease gun
erupted into space. Causing your tool bag to slip

beyond the reach of your white glove, when you were attempting
to repair the space station's solar wing. Thanks
for that clump of language—*solar wing!* One of the clumps

of magic shat out by our errors. And thanks
to your helmet camera's not getting smeared,
in the inch between your glove and bag—irrevocable inch—

we see the blue Earth, glowing so lit-up'dly despite the crap
that we've dumped in its oceans, a billion tons of plastic beads,
precursors to the action figures that come with our Happy Meals.

Precursors to the modern Christmas tree and handle of the modern ax.
Precursors to the belts and jackets of the vegans.
The cleanup crews call them *mermaid's tears,* as if a woman

living in the water would need to weep in polymer
so that her effort would not be lost/so that there would be proof
of her lament, say for the great Trash Vortex

swirling in the current, for the bellies of the albatrosses
filling up with tears that can't be broken down.
For the smell of mildew in the creases of ruptured beach balls,

for seabirds strangled by what makes the six-pack possible,
for flip-flops that wash up so consistently alone
they cause disturbing dreams about one-legged tribes

(described by Pliny before he sailed across the Bay of Naples,
into Mount Vesuvius's toxic spume).
Dreams logical, Heidemarie, given the fearful data.

Dreams had by us who live 220 miles below.
Queasy from our spinning but still holding on,
with no idea we are so brightly shining.

Not Housewives, Not Widows

Bad luck to enter the houses of old women, a commandment
broken when I entered their stone cottage, two streets over,
covered in vines that twirled around a rusted swing set
though they had no child. That they were witches: a conclusion

come to, given that they wore the clothes of men,
their wool caps covering their secret hair, their house
so laced in greenwork that it seemed continuous with the woods
and its nettles and the nickel in my pocket, which they paid

for bee balm I tore out of their yard and sold
back to them, the dirt-wads dangling.
"Don't let the birds out," muttered while I slipped
into the room with its stone walls, the backdrop

for a wounded jay who lived in a tin tub rattling with seeds.
Birdfeed, newspapers, feathers, guano—I saw
one substance splattering into the next in the life undivided,
windows open, birds flying in and out.

They worked their conjurations by feeding chopped meat
through a dropper, and wiped their hands
onto their jeans so you could see their long black fingers
streaking up the whole length of their thighs.

Freak-Out

Mine have occurred in empty houses
down whose dark paneling I dragged my fingernails—

though big-box stores have also played their parts,
as well as entrances to indistinct commercial buildings,

cubes of space between glass yellowing like onion skin,
making my freak-out obscure.

     ～

Suddenly the head is being held between the hands
arranged in one of the conventional configurations:

hands on ears or hands on eyes
or both stacked on the forehead

as if to squeeze the wailing out,
as if the head were being juiced.

     ～

The freak-out wants wide open space,
though the rules call for containment—

there are the genuine police to be considered,
which is why I recommend the empty vestibule

though there is something to be said for freaking-out
if the meadow is willing to have you

facedown in it,
mouth open to the dry summer dirt.

When my friend was freaking-out inside my car, I said
she was sitting in the freak-out's throne,

which is love's throne, too, so many fluids
from within the body on display

outside the body until the chin gleams
like the extended shy head of a snail! Even

without streetlamps, even in the purplish
penumbra of the candelabra of the firs.

My friend was freaking-out about her freak-outs,
which happened in the produce aisle;

I said: oh yeah at night, it's very
freak-inducing when the fluorescent lights

arrest you to make their interrogation! Asking
why you can't be more like the cabbages,

stacked precariously
yet so cool and self-contained,

or like the peppers who go through life
untroubled by their freaky whorls.

What passes through the distillery of anguish
is the tear without the sting of salt—dripping

to fill the test tube of the body
not with monster potion but the H Two… oh, forget it…

that comes when the self is spent.
How many battles would remain

in the fetal pose if the men who rule would rip
their wool suits from their chests like girls

in olden Greece? If the bomberesses
stopped to lay their brows down on a melon.

If the torturer would only
beat the dashboard with his fists.

Maypole

Now the tanagers have returned to my dead plum tree—
they sip the pond through narrow beaks.
Orange and yellow, this recurrence
that comes with each year's baby leaves.
And if the tree is a church and spring is Sunday,
then the birds are fancy hats of women breaking into song.

Or say the tree is an old car whose tank is full,
then the birds are the girls on a joyride
crammed in its seats. Or if the tree is the carnival
lighting the tarmac of the abandoned mall by the freeway,
then the birds are the men with pocketknives
who erect its Ferris wheel.

Or say the tree is the boat that chugs into port
to fill its hold and deck with logs,
then the birds are the Russian sailors who
rise in the morning in the streets where they've slept,
rubbing their heads and muttering
these words that no one understands.

Matins

Every morning I put on my father's shirt
whose sleeves have come unraveled—
the tag inside the collar though
is strangely unabraded, it says
Traditionalist
one hundred per cent cotton
made in Mauritius

Which suddenly I see is a haiku
containing the requisite syllables and even
a seasonal image
if you consider balmy Mauritius
with its pineapples and sugarcane.
And this precision sends me off
down the dirt road of my fantasy
wherein my father searched
throughout the store to find this shirt
to send an arrow from before the grave
to exit on the other side of it,
the way Bashō wrote his death poem:
On a journey, ill
my dream goes wandering
over withered fields

It suits my father to have hunted down
a ready-made for his own poem,
not having much of an Eastern sensibility,
having been stationed in China during the war and hating it
despite the natural beauty of Kunming.

They say a man dies when the last person
with a memory of him dies off, or maybe
he dies when his last shirt falls to ruin. Now
its cuffs show the dirty facing all the way around
and a three-inch strip of checkered flannel dangles down
into my breakfast cereal:
I have debated many days but
here it goes—
snip

and am overcome by an Asian wash of sadness.

Because the washer spins so violently, like time—
perhaps its agitations can be better withstood
with the last-memory theory, which means that a dead man
reposes longest in the toddlers that he knew,
which often are not many,
children being afraid of old men,
what with their sputum-clearing rasps
and their propensity for latching on to cheeks,
though my father was not much of a child-cheek-pincher,
not that he had anything against them;
he had a grandson he tolerated
crawling under the table at La Manda's
where between forkfuls of scungilli
as his kidneys chugged with insufficient vim,
he composed his other death poem,
the one that came in his own words, it went

Soon I must cross
the icy sidewalk—
help. There goes my shoe

Black Transit

Trees bare. Days short. And at dusk
crows pour through the sky in strands.
From a point in the east too small
to feed your eye on, they pop
into being as sharp dark stars, and then
are large, and then are here, pouring west.
Something chilling about it,
though they are birds like any birds.

What's fishy is the orchestration, all of them
with a portion of the one same mind: they fly
as if the path were laid, as if
there were runnels in the air, molding
their way to the roost. Whose location
no one seems to know—if they did,
you'd think there would be chitchat
in the market about the volume
of their screams, as if women were being
dragged by the hair through the woods
at night. But everybody keeps mum—
it seems we're in cahoots with them
without knowing what's the leverage
they possess (though we can feel it)
to extract from us this pact, this vow.

Heronry

Now my body has become so stylish in the ancient way—didn't Oedipus
        also have a bloated foot? Yes,
I remember him tied by the ankle in a tree, after his father heard the terrible
        prophecy and left him hanging
for the animals to peck and lap, same way the dog likes to lap my bloated foot
        when I take off the special socks
meant to squeeze it down. He likes to eat my epidermal cells before they fly
        off on the air that moves on through
the tallest trees one valley south, where great blue herons build their nests
        and ride on small twigs up—then gently
do their legs glide down my binoculars' field of view. The twigs they ride on
        never crack; how do they calculate
the tensile strength of cellulose versus their hollow bones? I thought of this
        at the hospital cafeteria
as I stared down an oldish woman's half-cubit of shanklebone, exposed
        between her sock and slack: it was
oldish skin I lapped until scowled at by her companion, who reached to the hem
        of her pant-leg and for the sake of what
rule of decorum gently pulled it down?

Les Dauphins

The dogs of the childless are barely dogs.
From tufted pillows, they rule the kingdom.
They'd stand for their portraits
in velvet suits, if they had suits—
holding hats with giant feathers.

And ousting the question: who loves the dog more?
the question becomes: who does the dog love?
The woman says: you are the one who plays him
a drum, you tap the anthem on his head.
No, the man says, you debone him the hen,
you tie the bow of his cravat.

The dogs of the childless sleep crosswise in bed,
from human hip to human hip—a canine wire
completes the circuit. The man says: I wonder
what runs through his head
when he squeaks and snorls all through his dream?
And the woman says: out
of the dream, I'm in his dream,
riding the hunt in my lovely saddle.

When the masters are gone, the dogs of the childless
stand in the mirror with swords on their hips.
They'd stand for their portraits with dogs of their own
if we were kings, if they weren't dogs.

Rashomon

Light passing through the leaves obliterates the subtitles
when the thief overtakes the swordsman
and forces his bride to submit. This is why

I need a new 42-inch flat-screen TV—
so I can read the dialogue of foreign films
that will improve me, though frankly it is horrible

to see the swordsman tied up and to watch him watch
the change in his wife's fingers
on the thief's (somewhat doughy) back. First

it looks as if she's fighting him, but then
she seems to pull him close,
saying *Now I am stained and must be killed* or

How do whales strain such tiny krill—these problems
of interpretation can be solved by money:
we need larger words. I have not abandoned words

even if with trepidation I now enter
the kind of store where they sell plastic polygons
that hum and blink. As the swordsman's wife

enters the forest on her pony, her trepidation draped
with a veil that renders even the biggest TV powerless
to show much of her face. But she shows the thief her foot

in its fancy flip-flop: that's what rouses him
to rape her in the leafy grove, I'll say what I saw
in the plainest words. I am not asking to be forgiven

for desiring 1080p, though I *am* asking
whether or not she asked for it: you'd think
we would have laid that one to rest (it seems

so strident, air-lifted from the 1970s
when I did not watch TV and also called myself a womyn—
a word it's hard to dress in a kimono) but apparently

we will never. At his trial, the thief (Toshiro Mifune)
sits wigwam-style in tethers and laughs maniacally
as he tells his version, though in somebody else's version

she's the maniac who laughs. We ask, but the new machines
refuse to say much more than this: that everyone
will get their chance to laugh and everyone

their chance to wield the knife—
be careful, it is sharp and growing
sharper, the more I spend.

Stargazer

When first I was given the one lily
chaperoned by two green pods,
I strapped myself in like a cosmonaut
to absorb the *whoosh* of seeing
its pods open one by one.

Because what mind cooked up such extravagance,
spot speckle pinkstripe smudge—
someone call a fire truck
somebody call a bomb squad
somebody call a pharmacist
for a Valium prescription.

Because the beauty of the world is soon to perish;
everything is burning up too fast—
lily number two goes off like a bottle rocket, leaving
the bloom and withering on the same stiff stalk
and the heart torn between them as the petals drop.

Oh, I might have asked for a simple daisy, something
to inflict a subtler vanishing…

without all this ocular pyromania
and the long-bones-dressed-up-in-a-coffin
scent. Plus there's one pod yet to detonate,
which the yellow pollen grains are trying to defuse

by lying scattered on the table,
precisely scattered on the wooden table
in a manner calibrated to this trapezoid of winter light.

The Unturning

for Ben S., 1936–2010

My friend said: write about the dog in *The Odyssey*—
four hundred pages in. I found him lying on a dungheap
where ticks sipped his blood, though in his youth
he'd taken down wild animals, eager to kill
for a man the gods favored! Who comes back
in disguise; you expect the dog to give him away
with a lick or a yip, but this is not what happens.
Instead we're told that "death closed down his eyes,"
the instant he saw his master after twenty years away.
And I wondered if my friend had played a trick—

setting me up with this dog who does not do much
but die. When the gods turn away, what can we do
but await their unturning? That means: don't think
that after so many years of having such a hard pillow,
the dog wasn't grateful. But I wonder
if, for the sake of the shape of the plot,
the author ought to have let him remain
for another line or two, if only to thump again his tail.

Wild Birds Unlimited

Because the old feeder feeds nothing
but squirrels, who are crafty and have learned
how to hang so it swings sideways until
gravity takes the seed—I bumble down

to this store of bird knickknacks and
lensware for the geeks, and while
the clerk is ringing up my Mini
Bandit Buster ($29.95), spring-loaded

to close the seed-holes when a heavy animal alights,
I read a pamphlet about bird-feeding, which I had not thought
was complicated, but turns out
is. Yes I bought the costly mixture

—not the cheap stuff full of milo—
which the birds kick to the ground, where it becomes
an aggregate of shit and chaff.
But I'd not known you must sweep it up

so as not to spread the pathogens, and space
your feeders far apart and dump
the seed each week and clean the feeder tube with bleach.
And you should whitewash the windows of your home

so the birds won't crash—you'll live in twilight
but your conscience will be clear. Otherwise
it's best not to feed the birds
at all: your help will only kill them, has killed them,

I killed them says Wild Birds Unlimited—thanks,
now let me tell you that your wind chimes
turn this place into a gong-tormented sea.
Outside, it's just another shop in the strip mall;

used to be that this place was a grove
of cedars where I knelt in the purplebrown duff
while something holy landed like a lunar rover
on my shoulder. But listen

to what sings in the grove's bright stead—
computer chips provide what you would hear here
if they weren't—mechanical birds
on plastic boughs, always flowering.

Bats

Light leaves the air like silty water
through a filterpaper sieve:
there is a draft created by its exodus
that you might think that if you rode
you too could slip away quite easily.

Is this why they call to mind the thought of death?
Squeak squeak, their song: I want to go
but I am stuck here, it is a mistake
being incarnate; I should be made
of the same substance as the dark.

If they must stay, like us they will be governed
by their hungers, pursuit
without rest. What you see in their whirling
is not purity of spirit. Only appetite,
infernal appetite—driving them, too, on.

Autothalamium

On my wedding night I drove the white boat,
its steering wheel a full yard wide. The dress
bellied out behind me like a sail
as I gripped the lacquered wood
and circuited the bay. The poem
by Akhmatova having already
been read, the calamari and cake
already eaten, I stood alone
in the wheelhouse while my friends
danced to the balalaikas outside
on the deck. I could not speak
for the groom, who left me
to the old motor's growl
and the old boards' groan; I also
couldn't speak for the moon
because I feared diverging
from my task to look. Instead I stuck
my eyes to the water, whose toxins shined
with a phosphor that I plowed and plundered.
And no matter what has happened since,
the years and the dead,
the sadness of the bound-to-happen,
the ecstasy of the fragile moment,
I know one night I narrowed my gaze
and attended to my captaining, while the sea
gave me more serious work than either love or speech.

Red Hat

I followed your red stocking hat
down the river of summer snow
until you carved the turn that stopped us both
with a spray of crystals. A prosthetic leg
lay on the ground, wearing a red
running shoe; we almost took it
to the Lost and Found, but skiing on,
we found more legs
perplexed the mountain. Leg
with thermos, leg with scarf, tableaux
with legs like bowling pins
struck down, though some were propped
erect, against a rock. Art installation
or object lesson?—first the body loses,
then it loses what it puts in place
of what it loses?—I thought
Mount Hood had come to life
to hammer this in. But I kept on
after your red hat and soon was overtaken
by one-legged men, a human wind
I whirled among for just a human minute.
Below, I saw them swallow you, then leave
you with the mountain shadowed on your back,
your red hat wagging, happily, it seemed,
despite the tons of rock you wore.

This Red T-shirt

was a gift from Angus, came with his new Harley
which no ladies deigned to perch their buttocks on
and was therefore sold minus the shirt—
net cost: three thousand dollars, I wear the money
in my sleep. The black braid flowing from the man

herding dice at the Squaxins' Little Creek Casino
cost me two hundred thirty-five, well worth it
for the word *croupier.* Work seven months on a poem,
then you tear it up, this does not pencil out
especially for my mother who ate potatoes

every day from 1935–41. Who went to the famous
Jackson Pollock show after the war—sure, she was a rube
from across the Harlem River, snickering
at the swindle of those dribbles until death squelched the supply
and drove the prices up. I've known men

who gave up houses worth half a million just to see
the back of someone whom they once bought diamonds.
And I've known women to swallow diamonds
just to amplify the spectacle of their being flushed.
The Gutenberg Bible—okay, I get that:

five-point-four million dollars for a book of poems
written by God on the skin of a calf. A hundred years ago
the Squaxins could tell you easily
who the rich man was. He'd be dressed in a red robe
made of epaulets from redwing blackbird wings.

The Wolves of Illinois

When I stopped along the road and climbed the platform that the
wildlife people built, I saw the dead grass moving. A darker gold that
broke free from the pale gold of the field.

"Wolves," said the man who stood beside me on the platform. On his
other side stood his wife and children, I assumed, dressed as if they'd
come from church,

a boy and girl, her scalp crosshatched with partings from her braids.
Note that this is my way of announcing they were black

or African American, I am shy not only of the terminology but of the
subject altogether

compounded by the matter of words, *black* being strong

if not so precise a descriptor—

and my being torn about the language makes me nervous from the
start. "Look at the wolves," he told his children

before dropping a quarter in the scope, which I didn't need because I
had my own binoculars

and know the names and field marks of the birds

(like the white rump of the marsh hawk),

so I include "the white rump of the marsh hawk" as it flies over the
field.

"Those are coyotes," I said

with pity for the man's foolishness? is there a correlation between my
knowledge and my pity?

(an inside joke: the marsh hawk's having been renamed the *northern
harrier,*

though *marsh hawk* is stronger).

Plus what about the man's pity for the white girl with *coyote* in her
mouth

—*coyote* in two syllables, the rancher's pronunciation,

when *wolf* is stronger. I wondered whether he was saving face before
his family when he said, "No, those are wolves,"

or did he only want his kids to feel the dangerous elation of the word?

I could not tell because they did not look at me, they who had come
from praying to a God in whom I don't believe, though I am less smug
about that not-belief

(could be wrong, I oftentimes suspect)

than I am about the wolves. Because I know the wolves were coyotes;

the wolves were coyotes

and so I said, "There are no wolves in Illinois."

"No, those are wolves," the man said, turning toward his wife who offered me her twisted smile, freighted with pity or not I couldn't tell, the pity directed toward me another thing I couldn't tell, or toward her husband

the believer in wolves

(at least he was sticking by them, having staked his claim).

In the autumn withering, the eyes of the children were noticeably shining, but I saw only the sidelong long-lashed white part of their eyes as they stepped up to the scope.

 "Check out the wolves," he said (the minutes ticking)

(the minutes nuzzling one another's flanks)

(the minutes shining in the farthest portion of the field

as whatever emerged from it entered it again).

Pharaoh

In the saltwater aquarium at the pain clinic
lives a yellow tang
who chews the minutes in its cheeks
while we await our unguents and anesthesias.

The big gods offer us this little god
before the turning of the locks
in their Formica cabinets
in the rooms of our interrogation.

We have otherwise been offered magazines
with movie stars whose shininess
diminishes as the pages lose
their crispness as they turn.

But the fish is undiminishing, its face
like the death mask of a pharaoh,
which remains while the mortal face
gets disassembled by the microbes of the tomb.

And because our pain is ancient,
we too will formalize our rituals with blood
leaking out around the needle
when the big gods try but fail

to find the bandit vein. It shrivels when pricked,
and they'll say *I've lost it*
and prick and prick until the trouble's brought
to the pale side of the other elbow

from which I turn my head away—
but Pharaoh you do not turn away.
You watch us hump past with our walkers
with the tennis balls on their hind legs,

your sideways black eye on our going
down the corridor to be caressed
by the hand with the knife and the hand with the balm
when we are called out by our names.

Samara

1.

At first they're yellow butterflies
whirling outside the window—

but no: they're flying seeds.
An offering from the maple tree,

hard to believe the earth-engine capable of such invention,
that the process of mutation and dispersal
will not only formulate the right equations

but that when they finally arrive they'll be so
...*giddy?*

2.

Somewhere Darwin speculates that happiness
should be the outcome of his theory—

those who take pleasure
will produce offspring who'll take pleasure,

though he concedes the advantage of the animal who keeps death in mind
and so is vigilant.

And doesn't vigilance call for
at least an ounce of expectation,
imagining the lion's tooth inside your neck already,

for you to have your best chance of outrunning the lion

on the arrival of the lion.

        3.
When it comes time to "dedicate the merit"
my Buddhist friends chant *from the ocean of samsara*
may I free all beings—

at first I misremembered, and thought
the word for the seed the same.

Meaning "the wheel of birth and misery and death,"
nothing in between the birth and death but misery,

surely an overzealous bit of whittlework
on the part of *Webster's Third New International Unabridged*

(though if you eliminate dogs and pie and swimming
feels about right to me—

oh shut up, Lucia. The rule is: you can't nullify the world
in the middle of your singing).

        4.

In the Autonomous Vehicle Laboratory
RoboSeed is flying.
It is not a sorrow though its motor makes an annoying sound.

The doctoral students have calculated
the correct thrust-to-weight ratio and heave dynamics.
On YouTube you can watch it flying in the moonlight
outside the engineering building with the fake Ionic columns.

I said "sorrow" for the fear that in the future all the beauties
will be replaced by replicas that have more glare and blare and bling.
RoboSeed, RoboRose, RoboHeart, RoboSoul—

this way there'll be no blight
on any of the cherished encapsulations

when the blight was what we loved.

     5.
They grow in chains from the bigleaf maple, chains
that lengthen until they break.
In June,

when the days are long and the sky is full
and the swept pile thickens
with the ones grown brown and brittle,

oh see how I've underestimated the persistence
of the lace in their one wing.

6.

Is there no slim chance I will feel it

when some molecule of me
(annealed by fire, like coal or glass)

is drawn up in the phloem of a maple
(please scatter my ashes under a maple)

so my speck can blip out
on a stem sprouting out of the fork of a branch,

the afterthought of a flower
that was the afterthought of a bud,

transformed now into a seed with a wing,
like the one I wore on the tip of my nose

back when I was green.

ABOUT THE AUTHOR

Lucia Perillo's fifth book of poems, *Inseminating the Elephant* (Copper Canyon, 2009), was a finalist for the Pulitzer Prize and received the Washington State Book Award and the Rebekah Johnson Bobbitt National Prize from the Library of Congress. Her book of stories, *Happiness Is a Chemical in the Brain*, will be published by Norton in 2012, and a book of her essays, *I've Heard the Vultures Singing*, is out in paperback from Trinity University Press.

Since 1972, Copper Canyon Press has fostered the work of emerging, established, and world-renowned poets for an expanding audience. The Press thrives with the generous patronage of readers, writers, booksellers, librarians, teachers, students, and funders — everyone who shares the belief that poetry is vital to language and living.

MAJOR SUPPORT HAS BEEN PROVIDED BY:

The Paul G. Allen Family Foundation
Amazon.com
Anonymous
Arcadia Fund
John Branch
Diana and Jay Broze
Beroz Ferrell & The Point, LLC
Mimi Gardner Gates
Carolyn and Robert Hedin
Golden Lasso, LLC
Gull Industries, Inc.
on behalf of William and Ruth True
Lannan Foundation
Rhoady and Jeanne Marie Lee
Maurer Family Foundation
National Endowment for the Arts
New Mexico Community Foundation
Penny and Jerry Peabody
Joseph C. Roberts
Cynthia Lovelace Sears and Frank Buxton
Washington State Arts Commission
Charles and Barbara Wright

To learn more about underwriting Copper Canyon Press titles,
please call 360-385-4925 ext. 103

The Chinese character for poetry is made up of two parts: "word" and "temple." It also serves as pressmark for Copper Canyon Press.

The text is set in Whitman, designed by Kent Lew. The heads are set in FF Acanthus Text, designed by Akira Kobayashi. Both typefaces are contemporary digital reflections on English and French typefaces of the 1780s. Book design and composition by Valerie Brewster. Printed on archival-quality paper at McNaughton & Gunn, Inc.